CW01043979

The Snail Who Couldn't Fly

***

A Tale of Sammy the Snail

written by

Cade McKay

and Illustrated by

CJ McKay

The Snail Who Couldn't Fly

First Edition: 2023

ISBN-13: 9798863685328

For all the children who feel pressured to be

different; being different is never a bad thing

The Snail Who Couldn't Fly

***

A Tale of Sammy the Snail

written by

Cade McKay

and Illustrated by

CJ McKay

Sammy the snail was a curious snail and decided his purpose was to explore new places, seek out new adventures and fearlessly slime where no snail had slimed before.

Until now he had only known leaves and mud and compost and the bottom of plant pots.

Sammy asked himself, "Am I always destined to slug along the ground?"

He thought there must be a bigger world out there.

He saw the birds flying and the fish swimming and decided today was the day to rethink his life.

He knew that caterpillars managed to change and could turn into something that could fly so why couldn't he?

He could see one now chomping at a very juicy leaf. Much nicer than those in the compost heap.

So perhaps that was the answer...to eat and eat ...and eat...until he turned into a butterfly.

So he tried eating the courgettes and the sweet peas and every new little leaf that came above the ground.

But no matter how much he ate he didn't grow any wings.

So he slithered further down the garden towards the pond.

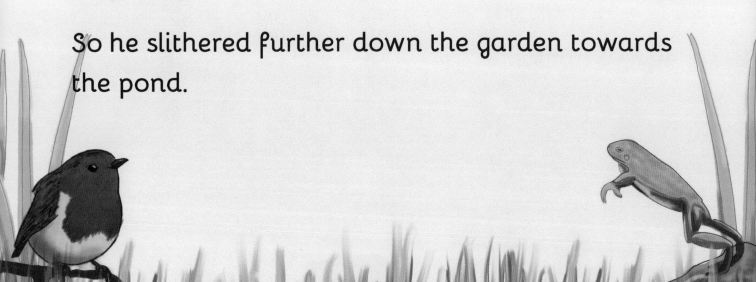

He sat by the water thinking what else to try.

He noticed the tadpoles that were slowly turning into frogs.

Frogs who could jump so far and explore so wide.

And he started to form a new plan.

Well, he thought, there must be something about being in water that helped one to grow nice strong legs so you could jump everywhere really fast.

But he thought the pond looked a little dark and deep.

After a while he remembered there was a nice puddle near the compost heap and thought that might do instead.

He dived into the muddy water and wiggled and swam just like the tadpoles.

When he got tired he floated across the water using his shell as a sail.

But try as he might he didn't grow any legs.

Sammy was starting to think he might need to try something else. He decided to give it one more try.

He had seen eggs in their nests. If they stayed warm and cozy they seemed to turn into birds.

So he looked around for a hollow in the roots of a tree which was just the right size.

He spent a long time gathering leaves and all sorts of things from the garden to make it really cozy.

He climbed in and slept for a long time.

When he woke he looked to see if he had grown wings but nothing had happened.

Just then an ant came scurrying along looking quite worried. He stopped to peer over the edge of Sammy's little nest.

"Oh," he said looking disappointed. "I was hoping to find somewhere to hide".
"Why what's the matter?" said Sammy.

The ant told him he was trying to hide from something big and nasty that was trying to eat him.

Sammy was scared for the ant and wanted to help.

He said, "I have a big strong shell, come and hide
in here!"
The ant rushed in and cowered under his shell.

A deep shadow passed over the nest but, no longer
able to see the ant, the shadow kept moving and
disappeared slowly into the distance.

The ant breathed a big sigh of relief.

"Thank you!" He said. "Now I can go back to join all my brothers and sisters. They will be so worried."

Sammy smiled and waved as the ant scuttled off among the undergrowth.

Sammy felt really happy that he had been able to help the ant and had a little rest.

It had begun to rain and Sammy peered up into the leaves as the drips fell through onto the ground.

He could see a little bird perched on a branch, not flying now, but looking quite cold and bedraggled in the rain as he fluffed up his feathers to keep warm.

The bird muttered quietly to himself, "Sometimes I wish I still had my little egg to keep me dry."

Sammy peered up into the rain that he loved so much, and then over his shoulder at the shell on his own back.

Then he looked up at the bird with sympathy. "Not only do I have a shell", he thought, "but I don't even mind the rain."

"Why don't you come and shelter with me,"
he offered.

"Really?" Said the little bird, "are you sure?"

"Yes of course," said Sammy.

So the little bird flew down and crept into Sammy's
little nest.

He felt nice and cosy sheltering against Sammy's
shell and stayed until the rain had stopped.

"Thank you," said the bird. "How lucky you are to have such a wonderful shell".

"Yes," said Sammy proudly, really pleased he had now helped the bird as well as the ant, "and I can curl right up inside it".

"You are really lucky," said the bird.

Sammy watched as the bird flew back up into the tree and thought about the shell on his back.

Sammy thought about what the bird had said and began to feel a little homesick.

He squelched out of the nest, slimed across the garden and slithered up a nearby wall.

He climbed right to the top of the wall and stuck himself to the underside of the eaves of the old empty house.

Sammy looked out across the garden and the fields; he could see the caterpillars munching the leaves, the butterflies skittering between the flowers, the frogs croaking in the pond and the birds flying between the clouds.

He thought about the quest he had set himself earlier that very day.

He thought to himself, "this morning I wanted to see the world and try different things. But then I started to want to BE different. I thought being a bird or a butterfly or a frog was better than being a snail, better than just being me."

Sammy considered how far he had slithered today, how high he had climbed up the wall, how he had helped the bird and the ant and how he could curl up anytime in his shell and stay nice and warm.

Sammy slithered a bit further along the wall and found a nice dark hollow where he settled down to sleep.

As he drifted into sleep his last thoughts were: "How content I shall be to shelter in my shell and explore in the rain and climb to the heights I can reach. And how much pleasure I can take in watching the ants work together and the birds fly and the butterflies wear their colours. What a great world we make together."

And his eyes closed into a deep sleep.

Published by Wilderhope Press 2023

Contact: wilderhope.wyn@yahoo.com